Dutch Ovens Chronicled

Sketches by *G. F. Zinkgraf*
Private collection photographs by *W. I. Bell*

Dutch Ovens
Chronicled
Their Use in the United States

John G. Ragsdale

The University of Arkansas Press
Fayetteville 1991

95 94 93 92 91   5 4 3 2 1

*This book was designed by C. H. Russell
using Optima and Revue typefaces.*

The paper used in this publication meets the minimum requirements
of the American National Standard for Permanence of Paper for
Printed Library Materials Z39.48-1984. ∞

Library of Congress Cataloging-in-Publication Data

Ragsdale, John G.
    Dutch ovens chronicled: their use in the United States/John G.
Ragsdale.
    p.   cm.
    Includes bibliographical references.
    ISBN 1-55728-220-X (c)
    ISBN 1-55728-221-8 (p)
    1. Dutch ovens--United States.
    2. Dutch oven cookery.
    I. Title.
TX657.K4R34   1991   91-18544
641.5'89--dc20   CIP

Contents

Illustrations

Acknowledgments

I thank the many people who played a part in supporting my efforts to assemble the material in this book—

My wife DeDe for continually editing my writings and assisting in my search for pertinent information.

Many librarians for assisting in providing books and information, particularly Nancy Arn and Irene Richmond of the Barton Library in El Dorado, Arkansas.

Preface

Dutch ovens as we know them today were developed in the early eighteenth century. They became standard baking vessels for early cooks on home hearths and fire sites. The size, sturdy cast-iron construction, and dependable heating made them a basic necessity which could be carried to cabins, campfires, wagon trains, and camping trails.

Seldom has a summary of the historical service of the Dutch oven been prepared. The following pages are an attempt to illustrate a revelation of the magnificent service the vessels have provided through the past centuries and continue to provide for us today.

John G. Ragsdale
El Dorado, Arkansas

1
Pots from the Past

From the seventh and later centuries we find references to cast-iron kettles or cauldrons ("kettle" 679–680, "pot" 1180). Even before that time cooks were using metal vessels for cooking on open fires.

By the sixteenth century, in Europe, rather routine cooking was done with cast-iron kettles placed on an open fire or suspended by some supporting structure over a fire (Tyler "Utensils" 29, Tyler "Vessels" 217).

The kettle is a metal vessel with straight sides, the diameter of which increases from the bottom measurement to the top. Kettles were often used as boiling vessels.

A pot is generally a bulbous vessel that narrows near the top and then flares out to a rim (Tyler "Utensils" 29). A pot is a stewing or simmering cooking vessel that can easily accept a lid. An early *Oxford English Dictionary* reference says that "pot" is the name given to the vessel that grows narrower towards the top, and "kettle" to the vessel that grows wider.

Both kettles and pots usually have ears near the rim, to support the lifting of the vessel. Some ears are vertical on the sides immediately below the rim, and some are at the level of the rim. Either type of vessel may have a permanent bail attached to the ears, or open ears which receive the hooks from a hinged pot hook. The ears of the vessels that date back to the seventeenth and eighteenth centuries were often angular in a "7" shape, and by the mid-nineteenth century some ears were rounded in a "cow's horn" shape (Tyler "Utensils" 31).

With the advancement of civilization in the fourteenth and fifteenth centuries, most households probably had several sizes and shapes of kettles and pots for cooking. Reports were made of pots carried by Columbus in his supplies on his journey in 1492 (Fears 94). We can certainly expect that an exploration group on an uncharted ocean venture would carry stored foods, livestock, and cooking pots to provide for the crew's food service.

Shakespeare, in about 1606, made reference to boiling kettles or cauldrons in the witches' scene in Macbeth—"fire burn and cauldron bubble" and also "in the cauldron boil and bake" (Shakespeare, *Macbeth* Act IV, Scene 1).

In 1620 when the Mayflower landed at Plymouth, the Pilgrim travelers had been cooking on board as they sailed. They carried brown sugar, oatmeal, oil, vinegar, dried peas, prunes, raisins, salt pork, dried beef. They also carried cheese, butter, turnips, cabbage, onions, parsnips, and spices. They built fires in sand pits on a lower deck and suspended cooking pots over them from the ship's beams. Obviously, with the movement of the ship, suspended cooking vessels would sway and detract from a constant heating of the pots (*Plimoth* introduction). Base-supported pots would remain stable, but the ingredients and liquids inside would slosh with the ship's movements. Probably in turbulent weather cooking was postponed. What unhappy news for the travelers and crews.

Until the start of the eighteenth century, in England iron was cast into molds of baked loam or clay soil. Drawbacks to this casting method were that the clay soil formed a rough mold and consequently the metal surface of the vessel was not smooth, and, what was more important, the molds were not well consolidated, and when the cast material was removed, the molds were usually destroyed after only one casting.

For many years, apparently, foundry technology was more advanced in the Holland area, and many cast-iron vessels were imported into Britain. These early pots were usually thick-walled and heavy (Tyler "Vessels" 217). In 1704 Abraham Darby traveled to Holland to inspect casting of some brass vessels in dry sand molds. From this observation, and after some experiments, he perfected a method to cast iron vessels in dry sand molds which used a better molding sand and mold-baking technique to provide smooth castings and better molds ("Darby" 492-93). In 1708 he received a patent for the process and soon thereafter began producing a large number of pots at his furnace in Coalbrookdale. By the mid-eighteenth century, these pots were being shipped to the Colonies and throughout the world markets ("Darby" 492, Tyler "Utensils" 29).

It is possible that the adaptation of this Dutch system for this patent may have led to some colloquial or even later reference to the Dutch pots. This is possibly the root for later references to Dutch ovens.

On through the nineteenth and twentieth centuries, pots were given descriptive names such as dinner pots, Gypsy pots, bean pots, stew pots, and stock pots, plus many local or family names.

Generally, pots made before the mid-eighteenth century were cast top down and had a sprue, a round projection, on the bottom from the casting method. Those cast after the mid-eighteenth century usually had a gate, a narrow line projection, on the bottom. This change took place over several years because manufacturers often are reluctant to change methods that have been in conventional use (Tyler "Utensils" 30). Both sprues and gates were formed when the molten metal was poured into the sand molds. After cooling and removal from the molds, the sprue and gate extensions were broken or cut from the cast vessel. By the end of the nineteenth century, better control in casting provided vessels without gates.

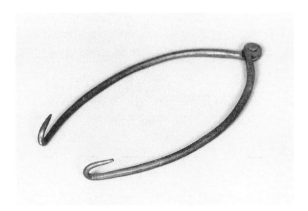

Hinged pot hooks were used by early cooks to lift kettles, pots, and Dutch ovens that had ears on each side. (Private collection.)

This pot came from Ireland as a utensil for the Museum of American Frontier Culture's model Scotch-Irish farm. It is the

5

type of pot that was in common use in northern Europe and the American Colonies in the early eighteenth century. The "7" style ears allowed the pot to be lifted with pot hooks, and the slightly recessed lid allowed coals to be placed on the top. The center arched handle provided for lifting of the lid. (Courtesy of the Museum of American Frontier Culture, Staunton, Virginia.)

This is a covered cast-iron pot with a round body, three legs, and a wrought-iron bail. The lid has a loop handle and a rim to contain coals. It dates from about 1770 to 1800. (Courtesy of the Philadelphia Museum of Art.)

2
The Hearth at Home

Bake Ovens

In the eighteenth century some open hearths were constructed with bake ovens. These bake ovens were auxil-
iary spaces for baking in the hearth area. The earlier
ones were box openings constructed in a side of the
brick or stone wall of the fireplace.

To use the bake ovens, a fire was started in the box space of the oven several hours before baking time. When the matrix wall of the brick or rock was sufficiently heated, the coals and ashes were raked from the oven and dropped into the fireplace.

After the food was placed in the oven, a door of wood, metal, or stacked brick was placed over the opening to reflect and retain the heat.

The food that needed the hottest temperature was placed in the oven first. When this was cooked and removed, another food item requiring a lower cooking temperature was placed in the oven ("Cooking" 47).

Later, bake ovens were constructed in the side of the fireplace facing the kitchen area. This was more convenient for the cook, who then did not have to lean over the hot, smoky fire in the fireplace to tend the fire or the food in the oven. Subsequently, hinged metal doors were made for the bake ovens. These doors opening to the kitchen made building the fire easier and also made it easier to place items in the oven (Goldenson 33).

A further development was a separate oven constructed adjacent to the fireplace. This was convenient and could also have been an addition to the existing hearth. These were sometimes called "beehive ovens" because of the shape, the bricks having been placed with a gradually reduced diameter from bottom to top. These ovens could be adjacent to the hearth, elsewhere in the kitchen, or even outside the house in a separate building (Goldenson 33).

Because of the hours it took to heat the oven and then bake the breads and pastries, baking was usually an all-day arrangement. Consequently, food was prepared and baking done to provide food for several days.

Some people refer to these ovens as Dutch ovens, but

the proper name is "bake oven," "brick oven," or "bee-hive oven."

Tin Kitchens

Tin kitchens were apparatuses used for cooking on the hearth. They were basically shaped-tin ovens that used reflected heat to roast meat or bake foods. The shapes, sizes, and designs were myriad. Adjustment of the cooking temperature could be made by moving the tin kitchen closer to or farther from the fire.

These tin kitchens probably gained wide usage in the late eighteenth century (White 46). Cooking on the hearth was common at that time, and the tin kitchen was considered a "modern" utensil. Many were used on into the nineteenth century when they were replaced by cook stoves.

The apparatus usually had a wide opening at the front, which was closest to the fire, with the top, bottom, or sides sloping to the back. If the bottom and the top sloped to a common point at the rear, and a tray or grill was in the middle, it sometimes was referred to as a "double-reflecting" cooker because heat was reflected both down from the top and up from the bottom. Some designs were a half cylinder, open on the large side which faced the fire. Many of the cookers had a hinged or sliding door at the back so the cook could view the back side of the food as it was cooking (White 47).

Some of the tin kitchens had a horizontally supported spit for roasting meat in front of the fire. Some of the spits were equipped with a handle on the side so the food could be turned more easily (Daniele 42). Many of the cookers had holes or channels to drain meat juices

9

during roasting. A pan underneath caught the messy drippings and allowed the dry roasting of meat.

These tin kitchens were sometimes mistakenly called Dutch ovens. They were more accurately "tin kitchens," "tin bakers," or "reflectors." They were very similar to our reflector ovens of today (Daniele 42). They were also known as "hasteners." Apparently, this referred to the meat roasting from the concentrated reflective heat, rather than the common spit roasting (Clair 209, 210, Earle 65, 66, Warren 90, 91). Today this same type of reflector is used by campers and some hearth cooks. With a blazing fire, reflective container walls, and a shelf for the food to be baked on, it can be very useful. It can also be disassembled, making it easier to carry, and reassembled easily.

3
Dutch Ovens, Then and Now

In the middle of the eighteenth century, the cooks of Colonial America were using many cast-iron vessels from England and some that were cast here in the Colonies. These vessels were generally used on the open hearths of homes or on fires in sheds or separate structures near the houses.

An improvement on the open pot was a close-fitting lid. A further advance was putting live coals on the lid to provide a concentration of heat at the top of the pot. Another refinement was the crimped or rimmed lid to retain the coals that were placed on it. These changes were gradual and mostly resulted from home design.

As the practical use and design of the Dutch oven advanced, the shape changed. Ovens became shallower, thereby allowing the cook to more easily place pans of food therein. Ovens also became wider, accommodating larger pans.

This Dutch oven, cast about 1800, is fourteen inches in diameter and three inches deep. It has sloping "7" ears and stubby legs. It probably served for many meals cooked on a hearth. (Private collection.)

From the mid-eighteenth century, Dutch ovens have been widely used. These ovens were used on open hearths during the eighteenth century and used on hearths and carried by settlers on pack animals or wagons on through the nineteenth century, and they continue to be used both on the hearth and outdoors today. The Dutch oven was often called a "bake kettle" or "bake oven." In recent manufacturing it has often been called a "camp Dutch oven"; this probably to clearly distinguish it from a kitchen oven that has no legs and no rimmed lid.

This Dutch oven dates from about 1850. The "7" ears are near the rim of the oven, and the bases of the ears are thicker where they are attached to the oven. The oven is ten inches in diameter and two and a half inches deep. (Private collection.)

Comparing our present Dutch oven with the early models, both have the same three legs to support the oven over coals; both have a rim around the lid to contain coals on the top; both have a bail for lifting the oven; both have vertical walls which are slightly larger in diameter at the top; and both have a lid that has a handle and fits firmly on the oven rim. Both ovens have flat bottoms and slightly domed lids. However, Dutch ovens made in the twentieth century are made by automatic casting systems, and we have better quality control of the metal. Most ovens now are made with a bail of steel wire formed for permanent attachment to the oven body. One thing that hasn't changed is that we still have a versatile vessel for browning, steaming, stewing, frying, and warming foods. And we have a superb baking vessel, fired with coals from the hearth or camp fire.

The origin of the name "Dutch oven" is uncertain. We have noted Abraham Darby's inspection of Dutch casting in 1704 which led to his patent development in 1708 in England. This is possibly where the name originated. However, some people believe that early Dutch traders (Hughes 96) or sales representatives brought about the use of the name. Some thought has been that the ingenious Dutch settlers in the Pennsylvania area may have been responsible for the repeated application of the name to the ovens.

Hearth Ovens

From the time of the three-legged spiders and the trivet-supported pans, there came the design for a long-handled oven. I prefer to call these "hearth ovens" since the handle was used to place the oven in the hearth location for cooking. These are also known as "camp skillets." They continue to be produced due to their popularity. I find this type to be less easy to manage around the camp fire because of the handle protrusion. Storage and transportation of these ovens can also be troublesome for the same reason.

This eleven-inch diameter hearth oven was cast about 1905 by John White and Son of Memphis, Tennessee. It has the usual long handle for lifting and moving the oven. The lid has a loop-style handle. (Private collection.)

This hearth oven has a typical long handle for lifting and moving the oven. The lid has a bar-type handle on the top. (Private collection.)

Kitchen Ovens

Probably the greatest majority of ovens sold to and recognized by the consumers as Dutch ovens are cast-iron or cast-aluminum pans with lids. Some of these ovens have ears on two sides, and some of them have a steel bail connected to the ears, although some models do not have ears or bails.

Earlier ovens were cast iron, but about 1889 cast-alminum ovens were introduced by the Griswold Manufacturing Company in Erie, Pennsylvania (Harned 12). These were widely accepted and continue to be sold today.

Many of the kitchen-oven lids are steeply domed and are self-basting. On the inside of the lid are concentric rings, circular patterns of protruding tips, or lettering that will cause moisture to drip back on the cooking food, or baste it, in a general pattern.

These sturdy pans with lids are used for stewing, soup making, boiling, and baking. They can be used on the stove top or in the stove oven. They serve as valuable vessels for multiple uses in the kitchen. I prefer to identify these well-used vessels as "kitchen ovens," even though often they are described as Dutch ovens by manufacturers, distributors, and consumers. They serve well in the kitchen but are not as useful for cooking on the hearth or at the camp fire.

Dutch Ovens

The true Dutch oven is a cast-metal container with three legs on the bottom. These legs allow the oven to be supported above the hearth or the ground and allow coals to be placed underneath. In the eighteenth century, some ovens had longer legs, similar to spiders or pots which were to be placed in the coals of a fireplace. Later ovens had shorter legs that were more satisfactory when placed over coals on the hearth or on the ground.

Some ovens were made with four legs; however, these are unusual (*Foxfire Appalachian* 2, *Foxfire* vol. 2 160). Three legs give more universal stable support. Miss Eliza Leslie commented in 1848 that ovens had three or four legs (Leslie *New* 402).

Some reports of earlier use of the oven recommended that cabbage leaves or other green leaves be placed on the bottom of the oven to keep foods from sticking or scorching, with the food placed either directly on the leaves or in another pan (Goldenson 38). I do not find this necessary. I simply oil the bottom of the oven with cooking oil, and food usually doesn't stick. If food does begin to scorch, it is often because there is too much heat below the oven. This can be controlled by adjusting the amount of coals under the oven. It is easier to control the heat if you do not place the oven directly on a bed of coals, but move coals from the main coals' source.

This oven has the logo "Phoenix Works" cast on the bottom and on the lid. The oven was probably cast about 1860. The ears are "7" shaped and are slightly thicker where their bases attach to the oven. The oven itself is ten inches in diameter and four and a half inches deep. (Private collection.)

18

Some early references mention putting a layer of sand or ashes in the bottom of the oven for a dampening or moderation of the heat (Leslie *Directions* 337). I believe this is excessive treatment and unnecessary if the coals under the oven are properly controlled.

If you wish to ensure some degree of protection for a pan in the oven, place three metal washers or two metal tent pins in the bottom of the oven, then place the pan on these supports. This will allow air to circulate around the pan, and the food will bake evenly at the oven temperature (Ragsdale *Dutch,* 1988, 8, *Camper's* 28).

Some early references to the use of the Dutch oven refer to the practice of placing the lid in the fireplace to heat it before use (Leslie *Directions* 337, Dick 250, *Foxfire* 2 161, *Foxfire* 8 91, *Foxfire Appalachian* 3). You should preheat the oven before baking in it. However, I find that placing the lid on the oven and then putting coals on the lid and under the oven preheats both adequately. Usually ten minutes is ample time.

If you are cooking on the hearth or very near a fire site, you may discover that one side of the oven is receiving more heat than the other. In that case, lift the bail and rotate the oven a quarter or a half turn. This is a good practice anyway in case the coals under the oven are unevenly distributed.

The lid of the oven has a slight dome, but it is not nearly as pronounced as that on a self-basting pan. The critical feature of the lid is the lip that extends up around the edge of it. This lip will retain the coals that are placed on the lid and will keep ashes from falling into the oven when the lid is lifted.

The coals on the lid are the key to providing the dry heat needed to bake items in the oven. When baking, about two-thirds of the coals should be on the top of the oven lid and one-third under the oven (Ragsdale

Camper's 29). Coals from the fire will gradually diminish and cool, so you should check the foods in the oven occasionally. If you observe that the baking items need more heat, additional coals can be added. Charcoal briquets give a more even heat than natural wood coals and usually continue to burn to depletion. When cooking with either natural coals or briquets, be sure to have additional coals ready to replace the depleted ones so you can maintain an even heat.

You can use the oven without the lid if you wish to brown, deep fry, or stew foods.

This nine-inch diameter Dutch oven was cast about 1880 by the D. R. Sperry Company of Batavia, Illinois. The vertical ears are a "cow's horn" shape (Tyler Antiques 221). The handle on the lid was cast separately and attached by a sealing, bolted connection. (Private collection.)

This twelve-inch diameter Dutch oven was cast about 1890 by the Bluff City Stove Works of Memphis, Tennessee. The vertical "cow's horn" ears provide for lifting the oven with pot hooks. (Private collection.)

Lid

The Dutch oven lid can be inverted and used as a griddle. Three metal tent pegs, rocks, or bricks make good supports for the inverted lid. The heat can be changed by varying the support heights or the amount of coals under the lid (Ragsdale *Camper's* 30, 31).

Another method is to invert the oven body and place coals on the inverted oven bottom and use the three legs of the oven to support the inverted lid. This arrangement has an unadjustable space for coals, but it can be used if no other support is available.

The lid of a Dutch oven should have a groove around the inside of the lid to insure a close fit when it is in place on the oven. This sealing of the lid joint is important to retain a slight pressure within the oven. Steam escapes from this lid seal when the pressure within needs to be released.

The lid must have a handle by which to lift it. This handle is ordinarily a looped cast piece in the center of the lid. Many early handles were cast from each side with a joint seam in the middle; some are still cast this way. This seam served as an indication of the center of the handle, thereby being a balance point for lifting the lid. Later manufacture of some ovens had the handle cast from one side, with the result that the handle was tapered from one side to the other. Some lid handles are cast as a solid flat, vertical extension in the center of the lid with a hole in the middle of the handle to allow lifting with a hook.

When any lid is lifted with a single pronged hook, care must be used to balance the lid and not spill the coals. One method for safe lifting with the single hook is to lift with the hook in one hand and tongs in the other hand to balance the lid. Another way to safely lift the lid is with a double-pronged lifter, which provides balance under the looped lid handle. A two-pronged piece of wire can serve as a lifter with an open-looped lid handle (Ragsdale *Dutch,* 1988, 4, 5, *Camper's* 26, 27). If no metal lifter is available, you can wedge a green limb in the handle and lift the lid.

Ears and Bails

Early Dutch ovens had ears on opposite sides to facilitate lifting them. The ears were generally of a "7" shape located vertically at the top edge of the sides of the oven. A hinged, wrought-iron pot hook would be inserted in the ears to lift the oven. The same hinged pot hook could be used on many of the pots in use on the hearth or fire site.

Some ovens were manufactured with solid mushroom-shaped ears on each side. These ears could be used with the hinged pot hook or a wrought-iron bail with a loop on each end. This looped-end bail could be slipped on for full-time use or could be used and removed after each cooking session.

Although early wrought-iron pot hooks could be used on several cooking vessels, this required the cook to place the pot hook on each vessel when moving it. The permanent wrought-iron bail was always in place. The only disadvantage was that it would sometimes become too hot to handle. These bails could be handled with a single hook or insulating pot lifters.

When necessary, the local blacksmith could repair or replace the bails. Since blacksmiths shaped malleable iron pieces, rather than working with molten iron, they didn't make cast-iron utensils, but they often designed or manufactured many other kitchen tools.

Currently, most ovens are cast with the ears horizontal and flush with the rim of the oven. Subsequently, a steel-wire bail is assembled in these ears. Some of the steel bails are made so that the bail will fall just below the rim on one side of the oven but will remain partially elevated above the rim on the other side. This partially elevated bail provides a handy grasp for lifting and moving the oven. The bail is usually flipped to the below-rim position during cooking time.

Care of Ovens

When you buy a new oven, it will probably be covered with a waxy coating, put on the oven by the manufacturer to protect it in shipping and storage. Wash the oven with detergent and hot water, rinse it, and let it dry thoroughly. Then coat it inside and out with unsalted shortening or cooking oil. You may place the oven on a flat pan in the oven in your kitchen at a low heat for a couple of hours (you should vent the kitchen during the heating). Remove the oven, wipe off any excess oil, and allow it to cool. This seasoning or sweetening will prepare it for use. You may also prepare coals on the hearth or in the camping fire and heat the oven with coals underneath and on the lid. After a couple of hours of heating, brush the coals from the oven and allow it to cool; wipe any excess oil from the metal. The oven is now ready to use. If the metal is not sealed, it may discolor food, and the food will be more likely to stick and burn.

If properly cared for, cast-iron Dutch ovens and lids are sturdy and should last many years to be heirlooms to pass on to the next generations, although cast iron or cast aluminum will break if it is dropped on a hard surface or receives a striking blow. Also, quick cooling of the oven may cause it to crack; therefore, you should not cool an oven by putting it in water.

Probably the worst hazard to cast iron is rust. To keep your oven from rusting, clean the surfaces which have been wet during cooking and rub them with a thin coating of unsalted oil or shortening. In the past, ovens were treated with animal fat, which was usually available. Shortening and cooking oil will both work equally well. Sometimes after long storage the oil rubbed on an oven will become rancid; if this happens, after you heat the oven for use, wipe the oil from the oven and apply a fresh coating.

To clean a Dutch oven after cooking, place about an inch or two of water in the oven and heat it to boiling; then scrub the inner area with a nonabrasive scrubber and discard the water and food particles. Repeat this once or twice to be certain the oven is clean. Never use soap to clean your oven since some soap might enter the metal pores. Allow the oven to dry and then apply a coating of shortening or oil to the surfaces that have been wet.

I usually just brush or rub the outer surfaces to remove ashes or dirt. If they become wet or show any signs of rusting, they should be brushed clean and oiled.

To store the Dutch oven, place it upright and set the lid ajar so air can circulate. Keep the oven dry and lightly oiled, ready for the next use.

Sometimes ovens or other cast-iron cooking vessels accumulate a layer of oil scale on the surface, either the inside or outside. This usually occurs because excessive oil or grease has remained on the oven and subsequent cooking baked it into a hard coating. Scrubbing or wire brushing will often have little effect on this scale. To remove the scale, build a large fire and place the oven in the fire, turning it occasionally so that each portion of the oven is exposed to the direct flame. This process usually burns off the scale, similar to the modern self-cleaning, high-heat kitchen oven. You can also clean any cast-iron utensil in a self-cleaning oven. The oily scale will be reduced to a dusty powder which can simply be wiped off.

Once the old oil scale is removed and bright metal exposed, the oven should be oiled, heated, and seasoned like a new oven.

Another alternative I have read of is to use a lye solution. This will not harm the vessel and will leave it ready for seasoning and further cooking use. Extreme care must be given to use of the caustic solution, however, because it can be harmful to the skin.

4
From East to West

In the eighteenth century, in the early years of our Republic, cooking on the hearth was the method most in use, from the massive stand-up fireplaces in the large houses to the smaller fireplace hearths of the general population.

Some of the wealthy families of English background had coal grates for cooking on the hearth. This was the continental method and was much desired by the genteel folk. This method of cooking was also desirable if the family had brought continentally trained cooks to this struggling land, since they could cook by the methods in which they had been trained.

Bake ovens were available in some of the more substantial homes. However, the vast majority of the colonists cooked on hearths and used wood fires, since wood was readily available. If the home had only a hearth, a Dutch oven or several Dutch ovens provided a ready manner to bake the meats and breads of the day.

In 1780 consideration was being given to a prisoner of war camp near Winchester, Virginia. Among the equipment requested for the camp were Dutch ovens (*Virginia* 387).

Mary Washington, the mother of General George Washington, wanted to be certain her cast-iron vessels were cared for. In her will, dated May 20, 1788, she provided that one-half of her "iron kitchen furniture" would go to a grandson, Fielding Lewis, and the other half would go to a granddaughter, Betty Carter. Surely there were several Dutch ovens among her "iron kitchen furniture."

As settlement of our country progressed, people took their belongings and customs with them. Their needs for housing, food, and clothing continued. The Louisiana purchase of vast lands to the west occurred in 1803. Subsequently President Thomas Jefferson led in supporting the Lewis and Clark expedition in 1804-1806 ("Lewis" 275). This review of our lands, backed by the Federal treasury, thoroughly planned by Meriwether Lewis and William Clark, was valuable in developing our United States. Reports indicate that one item in the equipment carried on the trip was a Dutch oven (Fears 94).

One account of life in 1834 describes an early home in Michigan in which the bake kettle or Dutch oven was the vessel in which the mother baked bread for the family. The reminiscence was one of fond memory of the steaming bread that was served (*Bark* 113).

Frances Phipps reports that in about 1840, Lora Case recalled their log house in the area of Hudson, Ohio. Case remembered that his mother baked rye and Indian bread in a bake kettle, or Dutch oven, set on coals with coals on the lid (Phipps 242).

A report of about 1840 in Indiana discussed the use of a Dutch oven. The cook provided red-hot corn pones or corn-balls for the guests (Hall 54).

Granville Stuart in the Midwest commented about his youthful era before 1845. In this time of tallow-dip candles and open fireplaces, the cast-iron skillet and Dutch oven were used for baking (Stuart 32).

Near Mt. Holly, Arkansas, Samuel H. Chester recorded many events in the lives of settlers developing the rolling, wooded hills of the area. A fond recollection of 1845 was the wonderful food from the "bread ovens, heated top and bottom with coals from the wood fire" (Chester 18).

In Maryland about 1850, loaf bread was baked in the ovens. After kneading, the dough was placed in a greased Dutch oven and the oven set near the fire to allow the dough to rise. The oven was then placed over coals and coals were put on the top. The coals on top were to be renewed frequently (Lea 58, 59).

In the 1850s Marion E. Watkins wrote about life in a log cabin near Mena, Arkansas. Among her recollections was one of the preparation of corn for the cooking of pone bread. After the corn was prepared, the pone was baked in an iron skillet, or Dutch oven, which was set over a bed of coals with more coals placed on the lid so both the top and bottom would bake (Watkins 7).

Around 1850 many settlers poured into the Texas area. On wagons and carts, many families brought their household goods, including three-legged iron skillets with tight-fitting lids. These Dutch ovens, of course, allowed cornbread or biscuits to be baked each day (Hunter 3, 9, 12).

In the period from 1854 to 1890, the states of Kansas and Nebraska were being settled. This was the era when many sod houses were being built and communities were being established. One child of this late nineteenth century reported on the cornbread he remembered being cooked in a coal-laden Dutch oven (Dick 250).

An article in the *Harper's New Monthly Magazine* of late 1862 contained an account of a trip to Missouri, in which the travelers gave a report on the biscuits cooked in "the three-legged iron convenience" of a Dutch bake oven (Brewerton 464).

During the Civil War, soldiers were glad to get possession of a Dutch oven, in which they baked their beans, cornbread, or corn pone (Franklin *Hearth* 78).

Cora Pinkley-Call, of Carroll County, Arkansas, remembered the Christmas of 1879 when cookie dough was sweetened with sorghum syrup. These cookies were baked in a Dutch oven heated with coals from the fire in the hearth (Pinkley-Call 30).

An adventurous voyage down the Ohio and Mississippi rivers was reported in 1879. In the midst of a group of river workers, one was known for his bread which was cooked in a "flat-bottomed, three-legged, iron-covered" vessel—his description of his bake pan or Dutch oven (Bishop 145).

About 1880 in western North Carolina, reports were

made of guests staying in a cabin. The cornmeal was stirred for the dodger and was cooked in the "round skillet with cover," as they called the Dutch oven, set over a bed of coals (Zeigler 151).

As pioneer families arrived in the Western areas to settle, houses needed to be constructed to provide living quarters. Often the local materials of wood timbers, rocks, clay bricks, or sod were used for the buildings. The cooking utensils, however, were usually brought by the settlers. A visitor to a California shack or a Dakota soddie would find the same items, such as a bean pot, skillets, a flour barrel, and a Dutch oven (West 53).

An 1880 report of cooking in the Rocky Mountain area referred to a bake oven jammed in the coals. After oiling the vessel with bacon rind, the cook baked the bread in it ("Rocky" 128).

Practical Housekeeping in 1881 contained an illustration of a cast-iron Dutch oven. The Montgomery Ward catalog of 1895 illustrated the cast-iron Dutch oven in diameter sizes of 10", 11", 12", or 14" (Franklin *Hearth* 78).

Galen Rowell's article in *National Geographic* tells of Theodore S. Solomons seeking a route through the Yosemite Valley of California in 1892, traveling with a partner. Among the equipment they carried was a Dutch oven (Rowell 478).

Many reports have been given of Dutch-oven cooking on the home hearth in the Appalachian areas. The foods prepared were meats, soups, stews, cakes, potatoes, and the often-repeated baking of bread and biscuits (*Foxfire Appalachian* 2).

Ronnie L. Sanders remembered his early years in the Arkansas Ozark Mountains when bread was baked on the hearth. The homestead was in an area near Bull Mountain in the late nineteenth century (Berry 45).

Patrick Dunnahoo provides great detail on the cooking reputations of some of the pioneer women in the late nineteenth century. In the Ouachita Mountains of Arkansas, biscuits were often baked in a Dutch oven, using coals in the fireplace (Dunnahoo *Tol'able* 60). He has also recorded biscuit making in the Delta country of Eastern Arkansas in the late nineteenth century. Women often made biscuits or cornbread in the "skillet and lid" or Dutch oven (Dunnahoo *Cotton* 248, 249).

Arie Meadows of Macon County, North Carolina, related how her mother cooked bread in a Dutch oven. She also baked pies in her oven, preparing several and cooking them successively (*Foxfire* 8, 91, 92).

In *Hearthside Cooking*, Nancy Carter Crump verifies that the Dutch oven is probably the single most important item for hearth cooking. It has been favored for generations to bake breads and desserts, to stew meats and vegetables, and to brown foods. As a person becomes familiar with hearth cooking, the Dutch oven's versatility is more and more appreciated. With this most important piece of equipment, anything done in a modern oven can be duplicated on the hearth (Crump 23).

5

At Home on the Range

When the western range land and vast cattle country were being settled in the late nineteenth and early twentieth centuries, the Dutch oven was a standard cooking utensil. It was carried in the settlers' covered wagons, in the cattle-ranch chuck wagons, in the sheepherders' wagons, and on the pack animals of the miners and the mountain men. The oven served for making stews, steaming meats, and baking cornbread and biscuits.

James H. Cook recalled some years in the late nineteenth century when he and other cowboys were furnished the basic trail supplies, which included a Dutch oven (Cook 13). The photograph on page 47 reveals a ranch cook site about 1900 where Dutch ovens were in use (Cook 246).

Frank M. Canton reported a frontier trail camp where three apparent rustlers rode from a campsite as several cattlemen approached. They found a coffee pot simmering on the edge of the campfire and a meal consisting of antelope steak, onion, and potatoes, along with biscuits baked in a Dutch oven (*Frontier* 16).

From 1860 to 1890 was a time of long trail drives when cattle were constantly being moved from the grass ranges to the market to be sold for beef for the distant consuming population (Worcester introduction xiii). To support the cowboy crews in these drives, the trail cooks usually served beef, beans, and sourdough biscuits as the mainstays of the menu. The beef was readily available and the beans and biscuit ingredients were easily carried. Using an active sourdough starter, the biscuits were often daily fare that was welcomed by the cowboys (Worcester 74).

Credit is given to Charles Goodnight for constructing the first chuck wagon in 1866. His base was the hardware of a government wagon which had iron axles instead of the usual wooden ones. The bed was of seasoned wood with a chuck box built on the back. Extra sideboards were installed to allow stowing the men's bedrolls, and then bows were placed over the wagon to support a canvas sheet. Usually a wagon had a water barrel on one side and a box to carry branding irons,

34

tools, and horse-shoeing equipment on the other. The chuck box had shelves and drawers for storage of small utensils and condiments. The piece across the back of the box was usually hinged at the bottom and would fold down to provide a work table, held level with metal supports from the top or a prop board below. Some wagons had beneath the chuck box another box or shelf for storage of skillets, pots, and Dutch ovens. Stretched under most wagons was a rawhide hammock where buffalo chips or cow chips were stored for use when no wood was available. The hammock was often called the cooney, from the Spanish "cuna" or cradle (Gard 120, 121).

Dan Moore reported on some Arizona ranch area where most of the wagons for the cattle trails carried cast-iron ovens that were anywhere from ten to twenty inches in diameter. In some areas where mountain terrain would prevent wagons from traveling, Dutch ovens were brought in on horses or mules so that meals could be cooked for the range workers (Moore 3). Not too surprisingly, in one camp, the cook, who cooked using several Dutch ovens, was called Dutchy (Moore 23).

Ramon F. Adams used his vast knowledge of cooking on the trail and referred to the Dutch oven as the most important utensil of the cook. He points out the essential use of the oven to cook biscuits. He also expands on the use of the ovens to steam steaks and roasts. The use of multiple ovens at a cook site increased the volume and variety of foods for the trail hands (Adams 79, 80, 89).

In the late nineteenth century on the large XIT Ranch of West Texas, the Dutch oven was almost a necessity. Besides the conventional biscuits, the cook prepared beef, vegetables, and fruits in the ovens (Haley 152).

Seventeen western states support the National Hall of Fame in Oklahoma City. The intent of this museum is to illustrate many facets of the work and life of the cowboy in our range history. One display includes a scene of a chuck wagon, which was the vital cooking center for the mobile trail and ranch workers in the West. Included in the display are Dutch ovens, which were widely used to steam meat dishes and bake breads and cakes for the workers.

Bronc in a Cow Camp, an 1897 painting by the renowned western artist Charles M. Russell shows a bronco and rider crashing through the cooking area of the trail camp, upsetting the utensils. On the left side of the fire are two large Dutch ovens. One oven with the lid ajar is half-full of biscuits, ready for the cow hands to reach in and serve themselves. (Courtesy of the Amon Carter Museum, Fort Worth, Texas.)

The Camp Cook's Troubles, *a painting by Charles M. Russell, shows the turmoil in a range cook site caused by an uncontrolled horse. A Dutch oven containing biscuits is visible in the center of the area. (Courtesy of The Thomas Gilcrease Institute of American History and Art, Tulsa, Oklahoma.)*

The Quarrel *by Frederic Remington shows a heated quarrel at a western camp site. Dutch ovens can be seen in the foreground. (Courtesy of the National Cowboy Hall of Fame, Oklahoma City, Oklahoma.)*

In about 1898 this cattle crew gathered in Dawson County, Montana, for their meal. Several Dutch ovens are near the fire, lids ajar for serving. (Courtesy of The Montana Historical Society.)

42

44

This scene shows a chuck wagon and cooking fire in a Nebraska camp about 1900. The chuck wagon has the cook-box work table down and some wash pans inverted on the cook box. In the foreground are Dutch ovens and other service pans, apparently placed near the fire to keep the food warm during serving. (Courtesy of the University of Oklahoma Press, Norman, Oklahoma. From Come an' Get It: The Story of the Old Cowboy Cook, by Ramon F. Adams. Copyright © 1952 by the University of Oklahoma Press.)

About 1900 this family group was camping in the area near Littleton, Colorado. Their Dutch oven can be seen near the fire site. (Courtesy of the Littleton Historical Museum Collection, Littleton, Colorado.)

In this 1908 scene, coals have been raked to the side of the fire and placed under one oven. The cook is placing the coal-laden lid on to bake the food. Other ovens are nearby for additional use. (Courtesy of The Erwin E. Smith Collection of the Library of Congress on deposit at the Amon Carter Museum, Fort Worth, Texas.)

In this 1908 scene, a ranch cook is using Dutch ovens to prepare the crew's next meal. (Courtesy of The Erwin E. Smith Collection of the Library of Congress on deposit at the Amon Carter Museum, Fort Worth, Texas.)

In this scene of about 1910 one crew member is serving himself while the cook cleans the dishes. Dutch ovens can be seen near the fire, and two are also set back with lids removed. (Courtesy of The Erwin E. Smith Collection of the Library of Congress on deposit at the Amon Carter Museum, Fort Worth, Texas.)

6
CAMPERS

Boy Scouts

The Boy Scouts of America has been a very substantial contributor to the appreciation and use of cooking with Dutch ovens. Since this organization was started in the United States in 1910, camping and outdoor events have been a major part of the activity program.

True to the motto of "Be Prepared," emphasis was put on preparation of wholesome meals in base camp or on the trail. This subsequently included the use of the Dutch oven. In the *Fieldbook*, instructions and photographs give good examples of Dutch oven cooking (1967, 174-77). Troop camping, competitive events, and public skill shows have also been particularly useful in demonstrating the use of Dutch oven cooking.

Minor S. Huffman, in *Magic Mountains* , pointed out that he was introduced to Dutch ovens by a cornbread serving from a Dutch oven about 1930 (Huffman 13). Subsequently he reports that at the Philmont Scout Ranch in New Mexico, the first summer instruction in 1939 sought to bring historical, local skills to the Boy Scout participants in the camping program. This instruction included use of Dutch ovens to cook meals on the outdoor trail (Huffman 21).

In 1947 at Philmont, Dr. Ray Loomis began a systematic instruction for the Scouts in preparing biscuits and cobblers (Huffman 141, 142). Even today these are good items to prepare in a Dutch oven.

Since the Boy Scouts were founded, the neckerchief has been a uniform item. Uses of the neckerchief have included signaling, bandaging, lashing, and troop identification. The neckerchief is worn around the neck and is usually secured at the two ends by a sliding keeper ring. *Boys' Life* magazine often has illustrations and directions for construction of a neckerchief "Slide of the Month." One slide in the November 1983 issue featured a Dutch oven dinner, complete with beef roast and vegetables, carved and attached with glue (Koob 68).

In the July 1989 *Boys' Life*, a brief article pointed out the advantage of using the Dutch oven for good, simple meals (Ragsdale *Boys' Life* 59).

Since 1973, the Boy Scout equipment catalog distributed to registered leaders and Scouts has contained a *Dutch Oven Cooking* book. This simple book has been a resource for many troop leaders and patrol cooks (Ragsdale *Dutch,* second ed.). Many people today still remember when they had good Dutch oven meals in Boy Scout or Girl Scout organizations.

Outdoorsmen

As noted earlier, the history of the Dutch oven in America parallels the history of the country's western movement.

During the twentieth century, the Dutch oven has been much used by those who camp or hunt in more inaccessible outdoor areas. The Abercrombie & Fitch catalog of 1913 listed a Dutch oven with a 13¼" top diameter for $3.00 (Abercrombie 133).

Although campers and outdoor cooks have used the Dutch oven throughout the country, it has been most popular in the West, as we can see from the ovens in paintings, stories, and photographs of the nineteenth century. There are few published reports from the eighteenth century to provide a comprehensive historical record of the ovens' use.

Charles F. Saunders described the Dutch oven as a homely pot on three legs, with a close-fitting lid that is indispensable to most campers. He particularly relished the slow cookery of rice, hominy, oatmeal, and the camper's staff of life—beans (Saunders 54).

Canoers benefit from the use of Dutch ovens, and many guides of fishing float trips use Dutch ovens to provide fresh-baked breads for some meals at camp sites on shore. While the fishers are at work, the camp cook can prepare hot breads and provide a welcome meal for all.

Cooking below Ground

Many people have followed the practice of baking foods in a covered container heaped with coals in a pit below ground level. The techniques vary, but the method provides a concentration of heat for several hours. This is really a slow-cook method which allows a one-pot dish to be cooked with minimal supervision. The Dutch oven is a sturdy container with a tight-fitting lid and is ideal for below-ground cooking.

This method of cooking is not new by any means. Civil War soldiers in the 1860s used Dutch ovens to bake beans by placing the ovens in holes dug in the ground and covering them with coals (Franklin 78).

A simple method of preparation for below-ground cooking is to dig a hole about twice as wide and twice as deep as the oven, line the hole with rocks, build a large fire in the lined hole, and let the fire burn to a mass of coals. Remove most of the coals and place the oven over the ones left in the bottom of the hole, and shovel coals around and on top of the oven, keeping the bail vertical. Then cover the coals and oven with soil, rocks, or other covering material (Kephart vol. 1, 345–346, Ragsdale *Dutch* 1973 13–14, Tarr 151, "Deep" 228, Weiss 211–214).

After marking the fire site with stakes for identification, you may leave the site for several hours of hunting or other recreation, and the meal will be ready on your return.

59

Ted Trueblood, writer of outdoor camping and recreation articles, has often referred to this method of cooking. He regularly used his cast-iron Dutch oven for such cooking (Trueblood *Wonderful* 14, 15; Trueblood *Pot* 26; Trueblood *Camp* 118–120, Bock 30).

Food Cooked in Iron Utensils

Iron is an essential mineral in the human diet. According to a reputable contemporary dietician, "iron deficiency is widespread throughout the world and is probably the most prevalent nutrition deficiency in human populations." Cooking in iron vessels significantly increases the iron content of some foods, particularly those foods with a high moisture content, acidity, and longer cooking times (Brittin 897, 901).

Not only are the meals prepared in Dutch ovens tasty and satisfying, but they also have nutritional benefits as well.

7
The Iron Makers

Past

Ironworks were established as early as the middle of the seveteenth century in the northeast part of our country. Locations were selected near sources of iron ore and water for mill power. About 1650, cast-iron vessels were made in Saugus, Massachusetts (Eaton 463).

One successful ironworks was the Batsto furnace in western New Jersey, which was founded about 1766. An advertisement in the *Pennsylvania Gazette* of June 7, 1775, listed for sale Dutch ovens from this manufacturer (Schiffer introduction 27).

This is a Model 10 Chuck Wagon Dutch oven manufactured by the Griswold Manufacturing Company of Erie, Pennsylvania. This model was cast during the period of 1930–57 (Harned 43). The oven is twelve inches in diameter and five inches deep. The flared rim on the lid may have been to allow coals to be placed past the edge of the oven. The bail has been slightly squared to accommodate the flared rim (Private collection.)

From the more primitive manner of casting Dutch ovens in the early eighteenth century, this very versatile stewing and baking vessel began to be made by many foundries both small and large. The ovens continued to be widely used on the hearth until the introduction of the kitchen stove in the late nineteenth century, which diminished their use. However, trail kitchens and outdoor camp cooking have continued to support the use of Dutch ovens on through the twentieth century.

This oven is a Century brand Deep Camp Dutch oven, Model 12DCO, manufactured by the ASW, Inc./Century Products Company of Birmingham, Alabama. The oven is twelve inches in diameter and five inches deep. The handle on the lid is a vertical strap with a hole in the center so the lid can be lifted. (Private collection.)

Cast-iron vessels were made in many ironworks throughout the industrialized area of the country in the nineteenth century. Wherever raw materials and demand existed, many vessels were made.

Dating of cast-iron Dutch ovens is imprecise at best. Shape, ears, bail, and quality of casting must be examined. A few of the nineteenth- and twentieth-century manufacturers placed their names on the lids; fewer names were shown on the oven body. Even among the ovens manufactured today, most do not have a name or logo on the lid or oven body.

Griswold Manufacturing Company of Erie, Pennsylvania, was a leader in placing some combination of name, logo, size, or catalog number on its cast-iron products. Today this is a great help in identifying these ovens and other products.

Some of the earlier known Dutch oven names are:

Barrows-Savery
Barstow Stove
Bluff City Stove Works
Fischer, Leaf
Griswold Mfg.
Martin Stove and Range
Phoenix Works
P & B Mfg.
D. R. Sperry
John White and Son

Present

One current manufacturer is the ASW, Inc./Century Products Company of Birmingham, Alabama. Associated names for this company were Birmingham Stove and Range Company and Atlanta Stove Works. They began casting iron products in 1889 and probably cast their first Dutch ovens in 1902.

A catalog of about 1938 shows both deep and shallow ovens. Lids were sold separately.

Deep ovens:

Diameter, inches	Depth, inches	Weight, pounds
9	4 ⅛	7
10	4 ¼	8
11	4 ½	10
12	4 ¾	12

Shallow ovens:

Diameter, inches	Depth, inches	Weight, pounds
9	2 ½	4 ¼
10	2 ½	5 ⅓
11	2 ¾	6 ½
12	3	9 ⅓
13	3	12 ½

Currently, the ASW, Inc./Century Products Company markets Century cast-iron ovens with lids in these sizes:

Diameter, inches	Depth, inches	Weight, pounds
10	4 ½	13
12	5	19
14	5	24

This oven is a Century brand Deep Camp Dutch oven, Model 10DCO, manufactured by the ASW, Inc./Century Products Company of Birmingham, Alabama. It is ten inches in diameter and four and a half inches deep. This oven has a loop handle on the lid. (Private collection.)

Probably the largest manufacturer of cast-iron Dutch ovens today is the Lodge Manufacturing Company of South Pittsburg, Tennessee. This company began as the Blacklock Foundry in 1896, became the Lodge Manufacturing Company in 1910, and is still operating as a family-owned business today.

A catalog of 1902–03 shows Dutch ovens with the "7" style ears and no bail, which would require a hinged pot hook for lifting. It was possible to purchase lids separately.

A catalog of about 1910 offered the following:

Deep ovens with lids:

Diameter, inches	Depth, inches	Weight, pounds
8	3	7
9	3	9
10	3 ¼	12
11	3 ½	14
12	4	17
13	4	19
14	4	23

Shallow ovens with lids:

Diameter, inches	Depth, inches	Weight, pounds
8	2	7 ½
9	2 ⅛	8 ½
10	2 ⅜	11 ½
11	2 ⅞	13
12	3	14
13	3 ⅛	18
14	3 ⅝	22

This oven is a Model 12CO2A Camp Dutch oven cast by the Lodge Manufacturing Company of South Pittsburg, Tennessee. The oven is twelve inches in diameter and three and three-quarters inches deep. The lid has a loop handle. (Private collection.)

By about 1920 these same deep and shallow ovens were shown, in addition to a sixteen-inch diameter oven in the deep size. A new style was also shown with ears flush with the rim and a wire bail attached to the ears; this is close to the current style.

These ovens with lids were listed:

Diameter, inches	Depth, inches	Weight, pounds	Price, $
9	4	10	2.10
10	4 ¼	12	2.40
11	4 ½	15	2.82
12 ½	5 ¼	21	3.36

The ovens with lids are listed in the 1990 catalog:

Diameter, inches	Depth, inches	Size, quarts	Weight, quarts pounds
8	3	2	10
10	3 ½	4	13
12	3 ¾	6	20
14	3 ¾	8	26
16	4 ½	12	32

About 1889, cast-aluminum cooking utensils were made and introduced to home cooks. Among the many vessels produced were kitchen Dutch ovens (Harned 12). The lighter weight and bright appearance of the aluminum ovens made them popular.

Today cast-aluminum camp Dutch ovens are available with three legs on the bottom and a rimmed lid, to serve the outdoor cook. The lighter weight makes these ovens more convenient to carry than the cast-iron ovens. These ovens are also easier to care for since they don't rust and no oil coating is required.

One current manufacturer is the Scott Manufacturing Company of Cleveland, Ohio. Their twelve-inch diameter oven functions as a serviceable Dutch oven for outdoor cooking.

8
Ovens in Action

During the eighteenth and nineteenth centuries most families used Dutch ovens regularly as they prepared meals in their homes. Several existing historic museums today demonstrate Dutch-oven cooking to the public. These museums provide an introduction to Dutch-oven cooking with actual cooking at the sites. The hours and dates open to the public vary and warrant verification before a visit:

Arkansas

Arkansas Territorial Restoration
200 East Third
Little Rock, Arkansas 72201

Ozark Folk Center
P.O. Box 500
Mountain View, Arkansas 72560

Colorado

Bent's Old Fort National Historic Site
Highway 194
P.O. Box 581
La Junta, Colorado 81050

Connecticut

Mystic Seaport Museum
Highway 27
P.O. Box 6000
Mystic, Connecticut 06355

District of Columbia

Old Stone House
3051 M Street, N.W.
Washington, D.C. 20007

Georgia

Tullie Smith House
Atlanta Historical Society
3101 Andrews Drive
Atlanta, Georgia 30305

Westville
Highway 27
P.O. Box 1850
Lumpkin, Georgia 31815

Illinois

Clayville Rural Life Center and Museum
Highway 125
Route 1
Pleasant Plains, Illinois 62677

Lincoln's New Salem
Route 1, Box 244-A
Petersburg, Illinois 62675

Indiana

Lincoln Living Historical Farm
Highway 162
Lincoln City, Indiana 47552

Conner Prairie Pioneer Settlement
13400 Allisonville Road
Noblesville, Indiana 46060

Iowa

Living History Farms
2600 N.W. 11th Street
Des Moines, Iowa 50322

Kentucky

Shakertown at Pleasant Hill
3500 Lexington Road
Harrodsburg, Kentucky 40330

Louisiana

Hermann-Grima House
820 St. Louis Street
New Orleans, Louisiana 70112

Maryland

National Colonial Farm
3400 Bryan Point Road
Route 1, Box 697
Accokeek, Maryland 20607

Michigan

Greenfield Village and Henry Ford Museum
Dearborn, Michigan 48121

Historic Mackinac Island
P.O. Box 370
Mackinac Island, Michigan 49757

Minnesota

Historic Fort Snelling
Building 25
Fort Snelling, Minnesota 55111

Missouri

Missouri Town
P.O. Box 124
Blue Springs, Missouri 64015

Wornall House
146 West 61st Terrace
Kansas City, Missouri 64113

New Jersey

Israel Crane House
108 Orange Road

P.O. Box 322
Montclair, New Jersey 07042

New York

Farmers' Museum
Cooperstown, New York 13326

Fort Crailo State Historic Site
9 1/2 Riverside Avenue
Rensselaer, New York 12144

Genessee Country Village
Flint Hill Road
Mumford, New York 14511

Obadiah Smith House
Smithtown Historical Society
P.O. Box 69
Smithtown, New York 11787

Old Bethpage Village
Round Swamp Road
Old Bethpage, New York 11804

Richmondtown Restoration
441 Clarke Avenue
Staten Island, New York 10306

North Carolina

Tryon Palace
608 Pollock Street
New Bern, North Carolina 28560

Ohio

Hale Farm and Village
2686 Oak Hill Road
P.O. Box 256
Bath, Ohio 44210

Johnston Farm
Piqua Historical Area
9845 North Hardin Road
Piqua, Ohio 45356

Pennsylvania

Alexander Schaeffer Farm Museum
Schaefferstown, Pennsylvania 17088

Landis Valley Museum
2451 Kissel Hill Road
Lancaster, Pennsylvania 17601

Pennsbury Manor
Route 9
Morrisville, Pennsylvania 19067

Quiet Valley Living Historical Farm
Route 2, Box 2495
Stroudsburg, Pennsylvania 18360

1696 Thomas Massey House
467 Lawrence Road, at Springhouse Road
P.O. Box 18
Broomall, Pennsylvania 19008

Virginia

Colonial Williamsburg Foundation
P.O. Box 627
Williamsburg, Virginia 23185

George Washington Birthplace National Monument
Washington's Birthplace, Virginia 22575

Museum of American Frontier Culture
P.O. Box 810
Staunton, Virginia 24401

Turkey Run Farm
6310 Georgetown Pike
McLean, Virginia 22101

9
RECENT EXPERIENCES

As stated earlier, the Dutch oven can be used to brown, braise, or fry foods, but the classic use is for baking. The temperature in an oven is directly related to the amount of coals under and on top of it. I have measured temperatures up to 500° F, although they are usually in the 375-400° F range. Since the temperature is variable, or not as easily controlled as an indoor oven with a thermostat, you may need to vary the time the food remains in the oven.

I bake most foods directly on the bottom of the oven. However, to maintain control of cooking temperature, you may decide to use supports, such as a trivet, metal tent pins, or metal washers. You may also want to place the food in a pan on the supports.

You may use either natural coals or charcoal briquets. The heat inside the oven will be maintained when the coals are fully burning and will gradually subside as the coals mature or if the coals cease burning well. You generally can increase the heat by adding coals or reduce the heat by removing coals. Too much heat on the top or bottom will cause the food to scorch.

For an even baking temperature, place about one-third of the coals under the oven and two-thirds on the top of the lid. When using charcoal briquets, I usually place six to eight briquets under a twelve-inch oven and about fifteen to twenty on the lid. As the briquets age and are consumed, add new ones for long-cooking items. For foods cooking only thirty to forty-five minutes, the initial briquets will ordinarily last the whole time. If something needs to cook for several hours, each hour or so the lid should be dumped to remove the ashes that have built up and insulate the lid. Fresh coals should then be placed on the lid to continue cooking.

If you are using natural coals on your oven, the process is much the same. You may find that natural coals are consumed faster and do not have the constant heat retention of briquets. Cooking with them may require more vigilance.

For moving coals from the fire source to the oven, a small shovel works well. For briquets or large pieces of natural coals you may wish to use long-handled tongs.

Prior to placing food in the oven, wipe the inside with an oiled cloth and preheat the oven by placing coals underneath it and on top of the lid. (Usually ten minutes is ample time). Put the food in the oven and time the cooking.

Foods that can be cooked in a kitchen oven can be cooked in a Dutch oven. The temperature must be estimated, but experience, along with the guidelines given above, will help you learn to regulate it.

In a simple back-yard location or a remote camping site, a Dutch oven will provide the facility to prepare a warm, delicious meal. The following recipes illustrate the various ways to use the Dutch oven to cook meats, vegetables, breads, and desserts.

Baked Potatoes

Preheat the oven.

Select white russet potatoes and wash them. Prick the top of each potato with a knife blade or a fork; this will allow moisture and pressure to escape during baking. Prepare one potato per person to be served, or more if desired.

Place the potatoes on the bottom of the Dutch oven and bake for 45 to 60 minutes, depending on the size of the potatoes. Feel the potatoes to determine if they are mealy and ready.

Serve with margarine or butter and dillweed or other seasonings.

Biscuits

Hot biscuits are a simple addition to any meal. The dough for the biscuits can be made from a biscuit mix or from a scratch recipe. Here is my basic recipe:

3 cups	*flour*
2 tbsp.	*baking powder*
½ tsp.	*salt*
6 tbsp.	*cooking oil*
1 cup	*milk*

Preheat the oven.

Put the flour, baking powder, and salt in a bowl and mix. Add the cooking oil and milk to this mixture, and stir the ingredients together to prepare the dough. Put the dough on a flour-coated dough board or flat surface. With floured hands, knead the dough until it is smooth and then pat or roll it to a pad of about ½" to ¾" thick.

With a sharp biscuit cutter, cut the maximum number of biscuits from the dough and place the cut biscuits aside. Re-knead the dough scraps and again pat the dough to a smooth pad. Again cut biscuits with the cutter and place these biscuits with the others set aside. Continue this until all the dough has been used.

Remove the oven lid and place the biscuits on the oiled bottom of the Dutch oven. Replace the oven lid and bake.

After 10 or 12 minutes, lift the lid to see if the biscuits have cooked and browned on top. If additional baking is needed, replace the lid and allow the biscuits to bake longer.

When the biscuits are done, set the lid aside. Remove the oven from the coals, and bring it to the serving area. Recipe makes about 20 biscuits.

Coffee Cake

A welcome dessert at any campfire meal or on the hearth at home is a warm, tasty coffee cake. I have cooked these for breakfast or for an evening meal.

This is my favorite recipe:

1 cup	*whole wheat flour*
1 ¼ cups	*white flour*
1 tbsp.	*cinnamon*
1 tbsp.	*baking powder*
1 cup	*brown sugar*
¾ cup	*sugar*
½ cup	*cooking oil*
1	*egg, beaten*
1 cup	*milk*

For a topping, mix 1 tbsp. brown sugar and 1 tbsp. flour.

When I plan to make this on a camping trip or prepare it away from my usual kitchen supplies, I prepare my own cake mix. I use three plastic bags: one for the two flours, cinnamon, and baking powder; the second for the brown sugar and granulated sugar; and the third for the topping mixture. The other ingredients can be carried separately.

For this recipe I prefer to use a round removable bottom pan or springside pan for easy removal.

To provide support of the pan, I usually place two tent pins on the bottom of the oven. Instead of tent pins, you could use a trivet or three metal washers to support the pan.

Preheat the oven.

Oil the baking pan. In a mixing bowl combine the flours, cinnamon, baking powder, and sugars and mix well. Add the cooking oil, egg, and milk; stir the mixture well. Pour the batter into the oiled pan, and place the pan in the middle of the oven on the tent-pin supports.

After the batter has baked about 8 to 10 minutes, remove the oven lid and sprinkle on the sugar and flour topping. Replace the lid and allow the cake to finish baking.

Bake the cake for about 30 minutes altogether and test it for doneness by sticking a thin knife blade into the center. If the knife blade comes out clean, the cake is probably done. This test works no differently from its use in the kitchen oven, but may be slightly more valuable with the variable heat from the coals under and above the oven.

When the cake is done, remove it from the oven and run a thin knife blade around the inner edge of the pan to assure that the cake is loose. Then remove the cake on the removable pan bottom, or remove the sides of the springside pan.

This recipe serves 6 to 8 people.

Baked Squash

Select two medium-sized acorn squash. Wash them, cut them in half lengthwise, and remove the seeds. Preheat the Dutch oven. Place the halves in the bottom of the oven with the cut sides up. Put a teaspoon of margarine in each squash half.

Bake for about 15 to 20 minutes, then check for doneness by removing the oven lid and pricking the squash with a knife blade.

Serve the squash halves sprinkled with dillweed or grated nutmeg.

Serves 4 people.

Steamed Rice

1 11 oz.	can beef broth
1 ½ cups	water
1 tbsp.	margarine
2 cups	brown rice
1 tbsp.	parsley flakes

Preheat the Dutch oven.

Put the broth, water, margarine, and rice in the Dutch oven and stir. Cover and cook for about 45 minutes or until rice is tender. Sprinkle the parsley flakes in the rice and stir well; cover and let stand for two or three minutes.

Serves 6 to 8 people.

Oyster Casserole

This is a simple casserole to bake in your oven:

1 qt.	oysters
2 cups	cracker crumbs
4 tbsp.	margarine
1 cup	liquid

Preheat the Dutch oven. Drain the oysters and retain the liquid. Oil a baking pan. Place one-third of the cracker crumbs on the bottom of the pan, then cover them with a layer of one-half of the oysters, and add 2 tbsp. margarine. Repeat with a layer of one-third of the cracker crumbs, a layer of the other half of the oysters, 2 tbsp. margarine, and finally a layer of the remaining cracker crumbs. Add a cup of the drained oyster liquid. Place the pan in the Dutch oven; cover and bake for 30 to 40 minutes.

Remove the pan from the oven, and place it in the serving area. The casserole will serve about 6 people.

From *Camper's Guide to Outdoor Cooking* by John G. Ragsdale. Copyright © 1989 by John G. Ragsdale, Gulf Publishing Company, Houston, Texas. Used with permission. All rights reserved.

Beef Stew

This famous dish is actually a combination of several foods cooked for different amounts of time. The way to do this in one Dutch oven is to begin with the meat and add the other foods in sequence to finish the dish.

2 lb.	beef, cubed
2 tbsp.	cooking oil
1 tsp.	salt
1 cup	water
4	carrots, diced
1 tsp.	minced onion
4	medium potatoes, cubed
1 cup	green peas
1 tbsp.	parsley flakes

Brown the beef with the cooking oil in the open oven; then add the salt and water. Put the lid on the oven and cook 30 to 40 minutes. Check the meat to be certain it is becoming tender. Add carrots and onions, and cook an additional 30 minutes.

Add the potatoes, green peas, and parsley, and cook another 30 minutes. During the cooking, additional warm water can be added to maintain about one inch of liquid in the oven.

Check to be sure all the ingredients are done. Remove the lid, and place the oven in the serving area. This stew will serve about 6 people.

Cabbage and Corned Beef

This vegetable and meat combination can be a simple meal in your Dutch oven:

1	*medium-sized head cabbage*
1 11-oz. can	*cream of celery soup*
1 12-oz. can	*corned beef*

Preheat the Dutch oven. Wash the cabbage, remove the core, and cut the head into 8 pieces. Place the cabbage, soup, and one can of water in the oven. Bake for about 10 minutes. Slice the beef, and place it on top of the cabbage. Continue baking for another 10 minutes or until the cabbage is done.

Remove the lid, and place the oven in the serving area. Serves about 4 people.

Baked Eggs

This method of cooking eggs provides a variety of choices.

Preheat the Dutch oven. Oiled muffin cups are ideal for baking the eggs in, or you can place cup-cake papers in muffin cups, which makes cleaning up a little easier.

Put grated cheese, crumbled crisp bacon, Italian seasoning, dillweed, salt and pepper, or any combination of these ingredients in the containers.

Crack one egg into each of the containers. Put them on the bottom of the oven, and bake them for about 8-10 minutes or to the desired consistency.

Cobbler

This dish has been enjoyed by thousands of campers and Dutch oven cooks for many years.

1 29 oz. can	*sliced peaches*
1 18 oz.	*cake mix*
	margarine
	cinnamon

Preheat the Dutch oven. Pour the contents of the can of peaches into the oven. Add the dry cake mix on top of the peaches, and level it. Put five or six teaspoonfuls of margarine on top of the mix, and then sprinkle ground cinnamon on top of the mixture.

Cover and bake for about 45 minutes. The liquid from the peaches will activate the baking powder in the cake mix, and the result will be a delicious cobbler with a crunchy crust on top.

Move the oven to the serving area, and serve directly from it. This will serve about 8 people.

Pecan Pies

This recipe provides individual pie servings and is usually well received by pecan pie fans.

For the crust:

4 oz.	*cream cheese*
½ cup	*margarine*
½ cup	*whole wheat flour*
½ cup	*white flour*

Soften the cream cheese and margarine; blend with the flour. Divide this dough into eight equal portions. Press the dough to the bottoms and sides of eight oiled muffin cups.

For the filling:

¾ cup	*brown sugar*
1 tbsp.	*flour*
1	*egg, beaten*
1 tsp.	*vanilla*
¼ cup	*margarine, melted*
½ cup	*chopped pecans*

In a mixing bowl, mix the sugar and flour. Add egg, vanilla, and margarine; stir the mixture well. Stir in the pecans. Pour the mixture in equal amounts into the crust-lined cups.

Preheat the Dutch oven(s). Put the eight small pie cups into one large oven or two medium-sized ovens. Cover and bake for 35 to 40 minutes. Remove the pies, and allow them to cool.

The pies can be served in the muffin cups or a serving container. This will provide 8 servings.

Parched Peanuts

An old favorite snack to prepare in your Dutch oven is parched peanuts. Peanuts have long been parched on stove tops and hearth fronts, but the Dutch oven can be used for great results. The Dutch oven can be the focus of attention and produce a welcome snack as well.

Select raw peanuts in the shell and put them directly into the oven. Do not fill the oven over two-thirds full so that adequate air space remains between the peanuts and the lid.

Parch the peanuts for about 30 minutes. You should remove the lid and stir the peanuts approximately every 10 minutes to be sure the peanuts parch evenly. Test a few peanuts periodically to determine when they are adequately parched. When the peanuts are ready, dump them into a serving container.

From *Camper's Guide to Outdoor Cooking* by John G. Ragsdale. Copyright © 1989 by John G. Ragsdale, Gulf Publishing Company, Houston, Texas. Used with permission. All rights reserved.

Bibliography

Works Cited

Abercrombie & Fitch [catalog]. New York: 1913.

Adams, Ramon F. *Come an' Get It: The Story of the Old Cowboy Cook.* Norman, OK: University of Oklahoma Press, 1952.

ASW, Inc./Century Products Company [catalog]. Alabama: 1990.

The Bark Covered House or, Back in the Woods Again.. Ed. Milo Milton Quaife. Chicago: The Lakeside Press, R. R. Donnelley & Sons Co., 1937.

Berry, Earl. *Pioneer Life and Pioneer Families of the Ozarks.* [No publisher given] Printed by litho printers, Cassville, MO, 1980.

Birmingham Stove and Range Company [catalog]. Birmingham AL: [1938].

Bishop, Nathaniel H. *Four Months in a Sneak-Box.* Boston: Lee and Shepard Publishers, 1879.

Bock, Lee. "The Amazing Dutch Oven." *The Mother Earth News,* September-October 1980: 30–32.

Brewerton, G. D. "In the Buffalo Country." *Harper's New Monthly Magazine,* June-November 1862: 447–66.

Brittin, Helen C., and Cheryl E. Nossaman. "Iron Content of Food Cooked in Iron Utensils." *Journal of the American Dietetic Association* 86 (1986): 897, 901.

Calendar of Virginia State Papers and Other Manuscripts, 1652–1781, Vol. I. Arr. and ed. Wm. P. Palmer. Richmond: R. F. Walker, Superintendent of Public Printing, 1875.

Chester, Samuel H. *Pioneer Days in Arkansas.* Richmond, VA: Presbyterian Committee of Publication, 1927.

Clair, Colin. *Kitchen & Table.* London: Abelard-Schuman, 1964.

Cook, James H. *Fifty Years on the Old Frontier as Cowboy, Hunter, Guide, Scout, and Ranchman.* New Haven: Yale University Press, 1923. Rept. Norman: University of Oklahoma Press, 1957.

"Cooking in Your Fireplace." *The Early American Life Fireplace Book.* Ed. Deborah B. Halverson. Harrisburg, PA: Early American Society, 1980: 46.

Crump, Nancy Carter. *Hearthside Cooking.* Mclean, VA: EPM Publications, Inc., 1986.

Daniele, Joseph. "Roast Your Bird in Our Tin Kitchen." *The Early American Life Fireplace Book.* Ed. Deborah B. Halverson. Harrisburg, PA: Early American Society, 1980: 42.

"Darby, Abraham." *Dictionary of National Biography.* 1917, 1950 ed.

Deep-river Jim's Wilderness Trail Book. Boston: The Open Road Publishing Company, 1937.

Dick, Everett. *The Sod-House Frontier 1854–1890.* Lincoln: University of Nebraska Press, 1937, 1954, rept. 1989.

Dunnahoo, Patrick. *A Tol'able Plenty: Pioneer Farm Life in the Ouachita Mountains of Arkansas.* Benton, AR: Alright Printing Company, 1982.

———. *Cotton, Cornbread and Cape Jasmines: Early Day Life on the Plantations of the Arkansas River Delta.* Benton, AR: Published privately, 1985.

Earle, Alice Morse. *Home Life in Colonial Days.* Middle Village, NY: Jonathan David Publishers, Inc., 1898, rept. 1975.

Eaton, Paul B. "Iron." *Encyclopedia Americana.* 1983 ed.

Fears, J. Wayne. "The Dutch Oven Tradition." *Sports Afield,* October 1985: 94*ff.*

Fieldbook, second ed. New Brunswick, NJ: Boy Scouts of America, 1967.

The Foxfire Book, vol. 2. Ed. Eliot Wigginton. NY: Anchor Books, Doubleday & Co., 1972.

Foxfire 8. Eds. Eliot Wigginton and Margie Bennett. Garden City, NY: Anchor Books, Doubleday and Company, 1984.

The Foxfire Book of Appalachian Cookery; Regional Memorabilia and Recipes. Eds. Linda Garland Page and Eliot Wigginton. New York: E.P. Dutton, Inc., 1984.

Franklin, Linda Campbell. *America in the Kitchen from Hearth to Cookstove.* Florence, AL: House of Collectibles, 1976.

Frontier Trails: The Autobiography of Frank M. Canton. Ed. Edward Everett Dale. 1908. Norman, OK: University of Oklahoma Press, rept. 1966.

Gard, Wayne. *The Chisholm Trail.* Norman: University of Oklahoma Press, 1954.

Goldenson, Suzanne, with Doris Simpson. *The Open-Hearth Cookbook.* Brattleboro, MA: The Stephen Green Press, 1982.

Haley, J. Evetts. *The XIT Ranch of Texas.* Norman, OK: University of Oklahoma Press, 1953.

Hall, Baynard Rush [Robert Carlton, Esq.]. *The New Purchase or, Seven and a Half Years in the Far West.* Ed. James Albert Woodburn. Princeton: Princeton University Press, 1916.

Harned, Bill, and Denise. *Griswold Cast Collectibles: History and Values.* Elmwood, CT: PRS-Harned, 1985.

Huffman, Minor S. *High Adventure among the Magic Mountains.* Allendale, NJ: TIBS, INC., 1988.

Hughes, Stella. *Chuck Wagon Cookin'.* Tucson, AZ: The University of Arizona Press, 1974.

[Hunter, John Marvin.] *Cooking Recipes of the Pioneers.* Bandera, TX: Frontier Times, [1936?].

Kephart, Horace. *Camping and Woodcraft: A Handbook for Vacation Campers and Travelers in the Wilderness.* New York: Macmillan Company, 1921.

"Kettle." *Oxford English Dictionary.* 1933 ed.

Koob, Kenneth. "Slide of the Month: Dutch Oven Dinner." *Boys' Life,* November 1983: 68.

Lea, Elizabeth E. *Domestic Cookery, Useful Recipts and Hints to Young Homemakers.* Baltimore: Cushings and Bailey, 1851.

Leslie, Eliza. *Directions for Cookery in Its Various Branches.* 1848 rept. New York: Arno Press, 1973.

———. *New Cookery Book.* Philadelphia: J.B. Lippincott & Co., 1857.

"Lewis and Clark." *Encyclopedia Americana.* 1983 ed.

Lodge Manufacturing Company [catalog]. South Pittsburg, TN: [1910], [1920], and [1990].

Moore, Dan. *Shoot Me a Biscuit: Stories of Yesteryear's Roundup Cooks.* Tucson, AZ: The University of Arizona Press, 1974.

Phipps, Frances. *Colonial Kitchens, Their Furnishings, and Their Gardens.* New York: Hawthorn Books, Inc., 1972.

Pinkley-Call, Cora. *Pioneer Tales of Eureka Springs and Carroll County.* Eureka Springs, AR: 1930.

The Plimoth Colony Cook Book. Erath, Sally Larkin, ed. Plymouth, MA: Plymouth Antiquarian Society, 1957, second ed. 1964.

"Pot." *Oxford English Dictionary.* 1933 ed.

Ragsdale, John G. *Camper's Guide to Outdoor Cooking.* Houston: Gulf Publishing Company, 1989.

———. *Dutch Oven Cooking,* first ed. Houston: Pacesetter Press, a Division of Gulf Publishing Company, 1973.

———. *Dutch Oven Cooking,* second ed. Houston: Gulf Publishing Company, 1988.

———. "Dutch Oven Cooking." *Boys' Life,* July 1989: 57.

"Rocky Mountain Cookery." *Scribner's Monthly,* 1880: 128.

Rowell, Galen. "The John Muir Trail: Along the High Sierra." *National Geographic,* April, 1989.

Saunders, Charles Francis. "The Dutch Oven." *Country Life in America,* 15 July 1912: 54.

Schiffer, Herbert, Peter, and Nancy. *Antique Iron.* Exton, PA: Schiffer Publishing Company, 1979.

Stuart, Granville. *Forty Years on the Frontier as Seen in the Journals and Reminiscences of Granville Stuart, Gold- miner, Trader, Merchant, Rancher and Politician, Volume I.* 1925. Bison Books, 1977. Rept. as *Prospecting for Gold from Dogtown to Virginia City.* 1852–1864. Ed. Paul C. Phillips. Lincoln: University of Nebraska Press, n.d.

Tarr, Yvonne Young. *The Complete Outdoor Cookbook.* New York: Quadrangle/The New York Times Book Co., 1973.

Trueblood Ted. "Camp Cooking Made Easy." *Mechanix Illustrated,* October 1976: 118–20.

———. "The Pot That Does It All." *Field and Stream,* April 1971, rept. April 1986: 25–26.

———. "Wonderful Dutch Oven." *Field and Stream,* August 1960: 10*ff.*

Tyler, John D. "Cast Iron Cooking Vessels." *The Magazine Antiques,* August 1971: 217–21.

———. "18th- and 19th-Century Cast-Iron Cooking Utensils." *Early American Life,* April 1978: 29–31.

Warren, Geoffery. *Kitchen Bygones: A Collector's Guide.* London: Souvenir Press, 1984.

Watkins, Marion E. *Capitol of Polk County: Pioneer Life and Customs.* [Arkansas], [1958].

Weiss, John. *Trail Cooking.* New York: Outdoor Life Books, Van Nostrand Reinhold Company, 1981.

West, Elliott. *Growing Up with the Country.* Albuquerque: University of New Mexico Press, 1989.

White, Frank G. "Reflections on a Tin Kitchen." *The Chronicle of the Early American Industries Association, Inc.* 36, September, 1983: 43.

Worcester, Don. *The Chisholm Trail: High Road of the Cattle Kingdom.* Lincoln: University of Nebraska Press, 1980.

Zeigler, Wilbur G. and Ben S. Grosscup. *The Heart of the Alleghenies or Western North Carolina.* Raleigh, NC: Alfred Williams & Co., 1883.

Works Consulted

Athearn, Robert G. *High Country Empire: The High Plains and Rockies.* 1960. Lincoln: University of Nebraska Press, 1965.

Bashline, Sylvia. "Dutch Treat." *Field and Stream,* March 1977: 178–80.

Beverley, Robert. *The History and Present State of Virginia.* Charlottesville, VA: The University Press of Virginia, 1947, 1968, rept.

Blacklock Foundry and Lodge Manufacturing [catalog]. South Pittsburg, TN: [1902].

Bliss, H. H. "Dutch Bakery." *Outing,* January 1915: 430.

Carhart, Arthur H. *The Outdoorsman's Cookbook,* rev. ed. New York: The Macmillan Co., 1955.

Carlson, Verne. *Cowboy Cookbook.* Los Angeles: Sonica Press, 1981.

Carson, Jane. *Colonial Virginia Cookery: Procedures, Equipment, and Ingredients in Colonial Cooking.* Williamsburg, VA: The Colonial Williamsburg Foundation, 1985.

Carty, Dave. "Dutch Oven Treats." *Outdoor Life,* November 1986: 89–96.

The Common Sense Cook Book. New York: J. C. Haney & Co., 1867.

Cooper, Susan Fenimore. *Rural Hours.* New York: George P. Putman, 1850.

Culbertson, Molly. "From Coals and Cast Iron." *Country Home,* October 1990: 134–44.

Dale, Edward Everett. *Frontier Ways: Sketches of Life in the Old West.* Austin: University of Texas Press, 1959.

Dobie, J. Frank. *Cow People.* Austin: University of Texas Press, 1964.

Doney, Carl. "Dutch Oven Treats." *Outdoor Life,* November 1986: 57*ff.*

Dow, J. R. *Dow's Patent Sermons.* First series. Philadelphia: T. B. Peterson and Brothers, 1857.

"Dutch Oven Hot Picnics." *Sunset,* February 1978: 68.

"Dutch oven miracles . . . from Utah: Six cooks show what you can do with the venerable cast-iron pan." *Sunset* (Central West Edition), September 1988: 76–79.

Fieldbook, third ed. Irving, TX: Boy Scouts of America, 1984.

Franklin, Linda Campbell. *300 Years of Kitchen Collectibles,* second ed. Florence, AL: Books Americana Inc., 1984.

Garvan, Beatrice B. *The Pennsylvania German Collection.* Philadelphia: Philadelphia Museum of Art, 1982.

Graber, Kay. *Nebraska Pioneer Cookbook.* Lincoln: University of Nebraska Press, 1974.

The Great American Dutch Oven Cook Book. Michaud, Dick, Mike Kohler, Juanita Kohler, Wallace Kohler, and Pat Kohler, eds. Logan, UT: The Festival of the American West, Utah State University, [1985].

Haley, J. Evetts. *Life on the Texas Range.* Austin: University of Texas Press, 1952.

Harril, Rob, and Libby Averyt. "Pan De Campo: Outdoor Bakers Vie for Honors in San Diego." *Corpus Christi Caller-Times ,* August 7, 1988: 1*ff.*

Hasbrouck, Alice Jackson. *As Our Ancestors Cooked,* New Paltz, NY: Huguenot Historical Society, 1976.

Hines, Fritz. *Introduction to Family Camping.* Irving, TX: Boy Scouts of America, 1984.

Holm, Don. *The Old-Fashioned Dutch Oven Cookbook.* Caldwell, ID: The Caxton Printers, Ltd., 1970.

"Hot Dutch Oven Bread in Camp." *Sunset,* August 1978: 70–71.

Norwak, Mary. *Kitchen Antiques.* New York: Praeger Publishers, 1975.

"Old Dutch Oven Made New." *Good Housekeeping,* October 1919: 42, 43.

Peet, Louise Jenison, and Lenore E. Sater. *Household Equipment.* New York: John Wiley and Sons, 1940.

Pryce, Dick. "Dutch Oven Desserts." *Boys' Life,* February 1979: 38–39.

Reener, Fredric G. *Charles M. Russell Paintings, Drawings, and Sculpture in the Amon G. Carter Collection.* Austin, TX: The University of Texas Press, 1966.

"River-runner's Upside-down Cake . . . and Other Dutch-oven Miracles." *Sunset,* July 1983: 84–85.

Weaver, William Woys. "Open-Hearth Cooking: Why All the Fuss Over Hot Ashes?" *New York Times,* April 27, 1988: C3.

West, Elliott. *Growing Up with the Country.* Albuquerque: University of New Mexico Press, 1989.

West, James, and William Hillcourt. *Scout Field Book.* New York: Boy Scouts of America, 1944.

White, Stewart Edward. *Camp and Trail.* Garden City, New York: Doubleday, Page & Company, 1911.

Woodall's Campsite Cookbook. A Fireside Book. Ed. Marilyn A. Bartmess. New York: Simon and Schuster, 1970.

Index

John G. Ragsdale

is also the author of two previous volumes devoted to campfire cooking, *Dutch Oven Cooking* and *Camper's Guide to Outdoor Cooking*, the first of which has been widely used by Scout leaders and patrol cooks. In 1947 he received his B.S. degree in civil engineering from the University of Arkansas and has worked in the field of petroleum engineering in several states and Canada since that time. He currently resides in El Dorado with his wife, DeDe.